Food for Thought

PAULINE FRANCIS

Level 3

Series Editors: Andy Hopkins and Jocelyn Potter

Pearson Education Limited
Edinburgh Gate, Harlow,
Essex CM20 2JE, England
and Associated Companies throughout the world.

ISBN: 978-1-4058-8183-8

Published by Penguin Books 2004
This edition first published 2008

1 3 5 7 9 10 8 6 4 2

Typeset by Graphicraft Ltd, Hong Kong
Set in 11/14pt Bembo
Printed in China
SWTC/01

Published by Pearson Education Ltd in association with
Penguin Books Ltd, both companies being subsidiaries of Pearson Plc

For a complete list of the titles available in the Penguin Readers series please write to your local
Pearson Longman office or to: Penguin Readers Marketing Department, Pearson Education,
Edinburgh Gate, Harlow, Essex CM20 2JE, England.

Contents

		page
Introduction		iv
Chapter 1	A Change of Plan	1
Chapter 2	Food for Thought	7
Chapter 3	A Potato with Green Eyes	14
Chapter 4	The Lie	21
Chapter 5	Trouble in the Fields	31
Activities		39

Introduction

'OK, I'll keep my promise. I won't tell anybody, not even Kate. But I'm not coming with you and I won't change my mind. Don't ask me again.'

'I won't,' Anna said. 'You'll see that I'm right in a few years' time. But it will be too late.'

Joe is working on his uncle and aunt's organic farm in Cornwall. But when he arrives, a GM (genetically modified) crop is almost in flower. And it is very close to the farm! In his first few days on the farm, Joe has a lot to think about – a lot of 'food for thought'.

Are GM crop trials safe or not? Who is right – the government and its scientists, or the protesters who trash these crops? Only a week later, during a storm, Joe has to decide. Can Kate, the daughter of a GM farmer, still be Joe's friend? And will Anna, one of the protesters, still like him if he doesn't help her?

Joe's uncle's farm is close to one the most famous surfing beaches in the country. During his stay, Joe learns more about surfing – but also about the problems of modern life.

Pauline Francis lives in the south of England and writes books for children. Some of her titles are: *Drake's Drummer Boy* (1998), *Little Giant* (2001) and *Television Man* (2001). She also now writes for young adults.

Food for Thought was written specially for Penguin Readers.

Chapter 1   A Change of Plan

Joe was in his room when the telephone rang. It rang again, but he didn't answer it. He didn't want to speak to anybody. He sat there thinking.

'I thought Tom was a good friend! I don't want to go on holiday alone! I don't know what I'm going to do.'

When the telephone rang for the third time, Joe ran downstairs.

'Hello, is that Joe?' a friendly voice asked. 'It's Uncle Dave. From Cornwall.'

'Hi, Uncle Dave,' Joe replied. 'How are you? Do you want to speak to Mum? She's at work, but I can give her a message.'

'No, that's OK,' his uncle said. 'I want to speak to you, Joe. What are you doing this summer?'

'Nothing,' Joe said sadly.

'I've got a bit of a problem,' Dave said. 'We need some help on the farm. I broke my wrist yesterday.'

'Oh, dear. How did you do that?' Joe asked.

'I fell over the dog,' his uncle told him. 'I didn't know who I could ask for help. Then your aunt thought of you. Can you come and work for us on the farm for a few weeks, Joe? I'll pay you, of course.'

'I don't want to work on a *farm*!' Joe thought. 'I want to surf in the sun, away from all this rain!'

'Er . . . It's not . . . I don't . . .' Joe began.

'You don't have to decide now,' his uncle said, laughing. 'Why don't you think about it? And talk to your mother.'

'I don't think I'm the right person,' Joe said. 'But thanks for the offer.'

His mother arrived home later that evening. She looked at Joe closely.

1

'You don't seem very happy, love,' she said. 'What's wrong? Did you meet Tom?'

'He's changed his mind about the surfing holiday,' Joe told her. 'He's going on holiday with his girlfriend.'

'I'm sorry, Joe,' she said. 'What are you going to do?'

'Uncle Dave rang,' Joe replied. 'He's broken his wrist, so he's asked me to help them on the farm.'

'Poor Dave!' his mother said. 'It's the busiest time of the year for them.'

'It was brave of them to start an organic farm,' Joe said. 'But I don't really want to go.'

'You'll have fresh air and good food,' his mother said. 'And you haven't got any other plans now. I think you should go!'

'Mum!' Joe said. 'I'll do what I want. I *don't* want to be on a farm in the middle of nowhere. There won't be any young people or any surfing!'

'Dave and Jenny are only about eight kilometres from Newquay now,' his mother said. 'Don't you remember? You can borrow my car.'

'Newquay!' Joe shouted. 'It's got the best surfing beaches in the country! I'll go. They need help. And I'll have some free time to surf.'

♦

A few days later, Joe was on his way to Newquay. At first he took the main road because it was quicker. Then, about thirty kilometres from Newquay, he decided to get away from the heavy lorries. He remembered his last telephone conversation with his uncle:

'Take the road across Bodmin Moor, Joe. It's further, but you'll get a beautiful view of the sea from the top.'

He took a small road up onto the moor. Uncle Dave was right. It *was* beautiful. The sky was blue and white clouds hurried across it in the strong wind. The fields were full of sheep and there were farmhouses here and there on the hills. Yellow wild flowers shone in the sun. Joe stopped his car at the side of the road and got out. He smelled the air and it smelled as fresh as the sea.

Joe now looked towards Newquay, hoping to see its famous beaches. But he was still too far away. He got into his car again and drove until he reached the other side of Bodmin Moor. As he came closer to the town, big black clouds began to cover the sky in front of him. Then, suddenly, the sun came out again and there it was below him – Fistral Beach, the greatest surfing beach in the country, with its yellow sand and big waves full of surfers.

Joe wanted to go to the sea now, but he was already late. He turned away from the town, taking a small road to the west. At last, as it was starting to rain, he came to a gate with the sign: TREGONNAN FARM.

His aunt and uncle were waiting for him outside their small, white house. Dave was ten years younger than Joe's mother, but he was thinner and taller and his hair wasn't grey.

'Hi!' Joe said.

His aunt spoke first. 'Joe!' she said. 'We heard your car. It's good to see you again. You're so tall now!'

Joe looked around him. There were no other houses near the farm, and no lights except the one in the farmhouse. He suddenly felt very lonely.

His uncle came up to Joe and shook his hand. He looked at the surfboard in the car as Joe spoke.

'Hi, Uncle Dave,' Joe said. 'You didn't have a beard last time I saw you!'

'No, I didn't!' Dave replied. 'And *you* didn't have a surfboard! When did you start surfing?'

'Last year, at university,' Joe said. 'I had to borrow the money from Mum to buy this surfboard. I had an old Malibu one at first. It was easy to learn on. And it was great fun in small surf. But this one's better because it's so light.'

Joe picked up his bags. As they walked to the kitchen door at the side of the house, Joe was surprised to see five or six tents in the valley next to a stream.

'That's our field too,' Jenny explained. 'We use it to earn money from holiday visitors. We're not the only organic farm around here now and we can't always sell all our vegetables.'

'One of our guests sometimes helps us on the farm,' Dave said. 'She's arriving tomorrow evening.'

'She's from Stockholm,' Jenny said. 'You'll like her, Joe. She's a student too.'

Inside, the living room was warm and comfortable. A large grey and white dog was asleep on a sofa in front of the fire.

'That's Fin,' Dave said. 'Don't fall over her!'

'Your room's the first on the left upstairs,' his aunt explained. 'It's got a good view of Cloud Hill.'

Joe went upstairs to his room at the back of the house. From the window he could see across the valley to a big hill covered with young trees. The sky was getting dark now and the moon was rising behind it. At the bottom of the hill was a field of maize. It stood straight and tall, and the tops of the plants were red in the evening sun. There was a light in the valley and Joe could see the shape of a house.

'Supper's ready, Joe!' Dave called.

Hungry as always, Joe ran downstairs.

'So who owns that field across the valley – at the bottom of Cloud Hill?' he asked. 'There's a house there too. Is it one of the other organic farms?'

There was a long silence. Jenny went into the kitchen and Dave put some more knives and forks on the table.

'Ken Ladock – and his wife,' Dave said at last.

'Don't you like them?' Joe asked.

'We don't know them very well, Joe,' his aunt said as she carried a large dish into the room. 'They bought the farm last year.'

4

From the window he could see across the valley.

'They kept sheep in that field for the first few months,' Dave said. 'Then suddenly, they sold them. We soon discovered the reason. We read about it in the local newspaper. By law, they have to tell everybody that . . .'

'. . . that they're organic?' Joe asked.

His aunt laughed – a cold, unhappy laugh.

'No,' she said. 'Their maize is GM – genetically modified. I can't believe it even after all these weeks! If the wind carries its pollen onto our farm, it can change our organic maize.'

'All GM crop trials have to be a hundred metres away from other crops,' Dave said. 'And two hundred metres away from an organic crop. We don't think that's far enough. That's the problem. Nobody really knows.'

'It's special here,' Jenny said quietly. 'We've worked so hard. This farm is our life and *nobody* is going to change it!'

'Don't worry, Jenny,' Dave said. 'It's *not* going to change.'

'It is!' she said. 'This is much more serious than anybody thinks!' She shook her head. 'Sorry, Joe, you've heard enough about our problems on your first night here. Now, let's see if you like our vegetables.'

Joe looked into the dish in front of him. The skins on the vegetables were not smooth and clear like the ones he ate at home.

'I've never eaten organic vegetables before,' he said. 'They look different.'

'They're different because they're not full of pesticides,' Jenny said. 'They taste much better. Doesn't your mother buy them?'

'No,' Joe replied. 'She says they're too expensive.'

'We don't eat meat, Joe,' his uncle said. 'I hope that's OK.'

'Fine,' Joe said, but he didn't really mean it.

Much later, Joe lay in bed listening to the wind and rain outside. 'No sun, no girls,' he thought. 'And now no meat!'

♦

Joe was dreaming. He was standing on his surfboard at the top of a breaking wave. He began to ride down the side of the wave as the surf broke over his head. At last he was riding inside the wave and there was a loud noise in his ears. He felt the speed of the surf as the noise became louder.

It was Aunt Jenny knocking on the door! She came in carrying a cup of coffee.

'What time is it?' Joe asked, sitting up with his eyes closed.

'Seven o'clock,' his aunt told him, 'and it's still raining. You'll have to borrow one of Dave's warm jackets.'

Joe worked outside all morning in the rain, picking vegetables. His boots were soon heavy with water. Rain ran from the end of his nose.

'I hate it here!' he thought. 'I want some adventure in my life. What can I do?'

Chapter 2   Food for Thought

'I've got to take some boxes of vegetables to an organic shop in Newquay after lunch,' Jenny said. 'Can you come with me, Joe? I'll need some help to carry them from the car park.'

'Great!' Joe agreed.

As they drove along the coast to Newquay, Joe saw Fistral Beach again. The sea looked wild in the heavy rain. The waves were high.

'I always lived in big towns until I married your uncle,' Jenny said. 'I hated the farm at first. I missed the fun and the noise of the city. Now I love everything here – the big skies, the sounds of the sea and the birds.'

The vegetable boxes were heavy, but Joe enjoyed the walk from the car park. There were surfing shops in every street on the way. As he walked, he noticed the sea, grey in the rain, between the roof tops.

'I'm going to the bank,' his aunt said as they left the shop. 'I'll meet you here in fifteen minutes.'

Joe ran into a café opposite the shop, ordered two hamburgers with cheese and ate them with great enjoyment. He didn't see the girl sitting at the next table.

'Hungry?' she asked.

Joe stopped eating and looked up.

'Mmm,' he said. 'I'm staying with my aunt and uncle and they don't eat meat.'

The girl smiled.

'Do you live in Newquay?' Joe asked her.

'Not far away,' she replied. 'I'm living with my parents on their farm until I find another job. You're not from Cornwall, are you?'

Joe shook his head. 'I live in south London,' he told her. 'What did you do before you came back here?'

'I was working at a sports centre in Manchester,' she said. 'I don't have many friends in Newquay. My father moved here last year when he got married again. I think the farm was Helen's idea. Helen's his new wife. She's really nice. Now you know all about me, what are *you* doing in Newquay?'

'I'm working on a farm for a few weeks,' Joe said, 'but I hate it. Too many wet vegetables and no meat.'

'What do you do when you're in London?' she asked.

'I go to the local university and I still live at home,' Joe told her. 'But I joined a surf club so I can get away at weekends.'

The girl's face showed her interest.

'You surf?' she asked.

'It's my favourite sport,' he said.

'I started to learn in Hawaii,' she explained.

'You've been to Hawaii?' Joe asked.

'Yes,' she replied, 'on holiday. And yes, the waves are the biggest in the world – *too* big for me. I've been to Fistral Beach a few times, but it's not much fun alone.'

'Hungry?' she asked.

'We *both* need a day's surfing,' Joe said. 'What sort of surfboard have you got?'

'I haven't,' she replied. 'I came into town today to buy one. But I can't decide which one I want.'

'I'll help you,' Joe said. 'But I only arrived yesterday. I don't know when I have a free day. Why don't you give me your telephone number?'

'Great,' the girl said. She took a piece of paper from her bag and started writing. 'Try to be free on Sunday. The surf's going to be good.'

'I will if I can,' Joe said.

'Thanks. That's my number,' she said, giving him the piece of paper. 'I've given you the number for the local surf information too – or you can get the information from the Internet. And before I forget to tell you, my name's Kate.'

'I'm Joe.'

He was enjoying their conversation.

Suddenly, his aunt opened the café door. When she saw Kate, her face became angry. Then she went outside again.

Joe wasn't very pleased. 'What's wrong?' he asked Kate.

'Why don't you ask your aunt?' she replied coldly.

'I will,' Joe said. 'I'm sorry, Kate. I'll phone you.'

But Joe didn't ask his aunt immediately. He was too angry.

'I don't understand why you were so rude to my friend,' he said at last.

'I'm sorry, Joe,' Jenny said. 'But she's Kate *Ladock*. Her father owns the farm across the valley, the one with the GM maize.'

'That isn't Kate's problem!' Joe thought, still angry.

They drove the rest of the way in silence.

When they arrived at the farm, Joe went into the house. As he walked past the kitchen door, he could smell fresh coffee. He noticed a girl with long fair hair talking to Uncle Dave.

'Hello,' the girl said. 'I'm Anna. You're Joe, aren't you?'

He noticed a girl with long fair hair talking to Uncle Dave.

'Hi!' Joe replied.

'Her eyes are beautiful,' he thought. 'They're the colour of the sea. Perhaps this job won't be too bad!'

Anna answered all his questions politely. Yes, she loved Cornwall and Tregonnan Farm. Yes, she spoke English so well because her mother was English. Yes, she liked going to the beach. Joe imagined them surfing together.

Anna stayed to eat with them. Joe soon realized that she had a lot to talk about with his aunt and uncle.

'So, it's finally happened!' she said. 'There are GM crops near Tregonnan Farm! What are you going to do?'

'We've written letters to our local politician and to the local newspaper,' Jenny replied. 'Most of the people around here feel very strongly about it. But what more *can* we do?'

'Some people have already trashed a GM crop not far from here,' Dave said.

'When?' Anna asked.

'About a month ago,' Dave told her. 'They trashed a large farm near Bodmin Moor. The police caught two of them, but the others got away in time.'

'People are saying that one of them, a young man, works part-time in the organic shop in Newquay,' Jenny said.

'How much do you know about GM crops, Joe?' Anna asked.

'My aunt and uncle have told me what's happening at the Ladocks' farm,' he replied. 'I can't decide. It's difficult now for Uncle Dave and Aunt Jenny, but we've got to have changes. New ideas usually frighten people. Think of the television, the car, the computer. Some people thought *they* were dangerous.'

'But this is different, Joe,' Jenny said. 'We're talking about living things, not machines. You can rebuild machines if there are problems. But if a GM crop changes our natural plants, then it's already too late. There's nothing we can do. I welcome new ideas, but not this one.'

'GM crops are already here,' Joe said. 'Can we go back to our old ideas now? Perhaps we should just use GM crops safely. And they will help poor countries. The farmers will get a better crop – and a cheaper crop because they won't need so many pesticides.' He wanted to change the subject. 'Tell me about Stockholm, Anna,' he said. 'I've never been there, but . . .'

'We're discussing serious matters here, Joe,' she replied.

Joe took a potato from the dish and held it in front of Anna.

'OK,' he said, laughing. 'Here's some food for thought! Is this potato a fish or a vegetable?'

Anna looked very surprised. 'A vegetable, of course!' she replied. 'Why are you asking me?' She started to laugh. 'I've read about that too! Scientists have put a gene into some potatoes to stop them freezing in the winter. The gene comes from a fish that lives in very cold water.'

'Scientists are already asking to test it,' Joe continued. 'Look out for them in the supermarkets in a few years' time.'

Anna gave Joe a beautiful smile and he smiled back at her.

'Is there any place for organic food – for natural food – in this science fiction future?' Dave asked angrily.

'If GM food is grown, there won't be any organic farms in ten years' time,' Jenny said.

'They say that GM crops will be better for our health,' Joe said. 'They won't need so many pesticides.'

'Joe!' Anna said. 'I can't believe you said that! *All* pesticides are bad for us. And if everybody eats organic crops, we won't *need* GM foods.'

'But shopkeepers want GM food because it lasts longer,' Joe said. 'And they want to please their customers. If customers ask for organic food . . .'

'I'll send you to work for Mr Ladock!' Dave said, laughing.

'It's OK, Joe,' Jenny said. 'We've talked enough about it. You know what we think. Now, when are you going surfing?'

'I'd like to go on Sunday, if I can have some free time,' he replied.

He looked at Anna. 'Will she ask to go with me?' he thought. No, she didn't look at all interested.

'Kate Ladock wants to come with me and I'm going to help her to buy a new surfboard,' Joe explained.

'So you're going out with the enemy,' Anna said.

'Kate hasn't done anything wrong,' Joe said. 'Her father and his wife decided to grow GM crops, not her. She wasn't even living with him then.'

'She's his daughter,' Anna went on, 'and she's chosen to live there now.'

'Perhaps she has her own opinion,' Joe said.

'She's as bad as they are,' Anna said.

'That's not fair, Anna,' Jenny said. 'I was rude to Kate this afternoon, but I was wrong. We don't know *what* Kate thinks.'

'I'm sorry, Joe,' Anna said. 'I'm just so worried about the GM crop trials. That's all I can think about.'

'It's OK,' Joe said.

Joe suddenly felt happy. He was going surfing with a new friend who really liked surfing. And Anna?

'I like her a lot,' he thought. 'And perhaps she *will* come surfing with me one day!

Chapter 3   A Potato with Green Eyes

Joe didn't see Anna very much during the next two days. She was helping his aunt in the maize field and she took his place on trips to the organic shop in Newquay. He began to count the hours until Sunday. Kate was right about the weather. When Sunday came, the sun was hot and there was a light warm wind from the west. It was a perfect day for surfing.

Joe was tying his surfboard on to the top of his car when Anna found him.

'I've got to go into Newquay again,' she said. 'Can you take me?'

Joe was very pleased. 'I'm nearly ready,' he said. 'I'm meeting Kate in the café. Come and have a coffee with us.'

'I can't,' Anna replied. 'Sorry.'

Joe felt excited when he saw Fistral Beach again from the road. It looked so beautiful in the sun, but Anna didn't seem to notice it.

'I can't wait to get into the water,' he said. 'I love surfing. It's not just a sport for me – it's more a way of life. Why don't you come after...?'

'No thanks, Joe,' Anna said quickly. 'I think it's boring. Surfers talk about it all the time. There are more serious things in life to think about.'

Joe felt angry but he tried not to show it.

'How long are you staying at the farm?' he asked.

'I don't know,' Anna replied. 'How long are *you* staying?'

'About another three weeks,' Joe replied. 'Uncle Dave thinks his wrist will be better by then.'

Newquay was very busy because the weather was so good. There were people everywhere – shopping or just sitting in the sun eating ice-creams. Anna asked Joe to stop the car near the town centre. Then he parked the car and decided to look at some of the surfing shops near the café.

As he walked towards the main square, he heard voices shouting, 'Stop GM crop trials before it's too late! Stop now!'

Joe decided to find out what was happening. When he arrived at the square, he stopped in surprise.

The square was full of walking vegetables – people with large paper vegetables over their heads and bodies. Each vegetable was carrying a sign: STOP GM CROP TRIALS NOW! STOP NOW!

15

A potato walked slowly up to Joe. It was black and grey and a very strange shape.

'Do you want to eat me?' a woman's voice asked.

'No!' Joe replied. 'What's wrong with you?'

'I was growing too close to a GM potato,' the voice said. 'Look at me!'

'No thanks,' Joe said, turning away.

The potato followed him.

'If you want more information, just ask,' she said. 'We want as many people as possible to know what's happening around here.'

'I know quite a lot already,' Joe said kindly.

Joe walked to the café. As he waited outside for Kate, he suddenly saw Anna on the other side of the street. She was talking to a man with long brown hair. Joe got up and ran after them, but he lost them in the crowd.

Kate was waiting for him when he arrived back at the café.

'Sorry I'm late, Joe,' she said. 'I had something important to do before I came.'

'I just saw Anna,' Joe said, 'but I lost her. She works on the farm. I wanted you to meet her.'

Kate didn't show much interest. She started to walk towards the main road down to Fistral Beach.

'There's a new surfing shop in Fore Street,' she said. 'It opened earlier this year. People all over the world use it to buy surfing equipment on the Internet. Let's go there first.'

The shop was bigger than any of the shops Joe knew in London.

'This is a great surfboard,' he said, picking up a brightly coloured one with three fins, 'and it's in the sale. Look, it's half-price! It's almost as good as mine.'

'Well, it *does* seem a good buy,' Kate said. 'OK, I'll get it.'

'Great!' Joe said. 'Now let's get to Fistral Beach!'

The beach was very crowded.

A potato walked slowly up to Joe.

'Let's go over there,' Joe said, pointing to the far end of the beach. 'There aren't so many people.'

'There's a quieter beach around the corner,' Kate said.

'It's OK here,' Joe replied.

At last they sat down on the sand and started to prepare their surfboards.

'You can surf between the black and white signs,' Kate explained.

'What's that building on top of the hill?' Joe asked.

'A very famous hotel,' Kate replied. 'It's often used in television programmes and films. It's a pity there are sharp rocks just under the water there. The surf's really good.'

When they were ready, they walked out into the sea. As the water came up to their waists, they stopped. There were a lot of people around them holding their surfboards. They were all watching and waiting for the perfect wave.

Joe felt excited. The noise of the waves filled his ears. He held his surfboard tightly, ready to go. Suddenly, the water rose slowly around them and everybody started to jump onto their surfboards.

'Come on!' Joe said. 'It looks like a good one!'

He lay on his surfboard and kicked hard. Kate followed him. Joe felt the sun on his skin as he lay there. It was wonderful! The wave became bigger. He waited. From the corner of his eye, he saw Kate just behind him.

Suddenly, the sea began to lift his surfboard and Joe jumped to his feet. He stood with his left foot in front and his right one behind. He bent his knees a little. The wave rose above him, its surf almost breaking. Joe rode quickly down its side, and the speed took him back to shallow water. He waited there for Kate.

'I was surfing faster than the breaking wave,' Kate said. 'I lost speed and stopped.'

'If you do that again, turn at the bottom of the wave,' Joe said. 'Try to get back into it.'

The wave rose above him.

'I don't know how to turn,' Kate said.

'I'll show you next time,' Joe said. 'This is the best surfing I've done this year. I feel alive again!'

'You're good,' she said.

'You are too!' Joe replied. 'You just need more practice.'

Joe looked up at the next wave.

'It's going to be a good one!' he shouted. 'Come on, I'll teach you a bottom turn!'

They went out together to meet the wave and they surfed together down its side.

'Now watch me!' Joe shouted.

Joe bent his knees and pushed hard with his feet on the surfboard. He rode above the water, turned sharply, felt his knees go weak – and fell off his surfboard. He watched Kate. She made a perfect turn and rode down the wave again laughing.

'Good try!' Kate said. 'Better luck next time.'

They went back to the beach to watch the other surfers.

'It's great here,' Joe said. 'I can pick potatoes all day if I can come here in my free time.' He suddenly jumped to his feet again. 'Watch that woman, Kate!' he shouted. 'She's tube riding! My friend Tom started to teach me how to do it. You wait until the surf breaks over your head. It's like riding inside a tube of water. It's one of the most exciting things a surfer can do.'

'It sounds good,' Kate said. 'Thanks for coming with me today, Joe.'

'Thanks for suggesting it,' Joe said. 'I forgot to ask you. Did you see the protesters in the market square dressed as vegetables? I'm sure one of them was Anna. It had green eyes just like hers.'

'Oh yes, I saw them,' Kate replied, with a little smile that Joe didn't notice.

'What do you think about your father's GM crop trial?' he asked.

'Did Anna tell you to ask me?' Kate said. 'Well, it's really difficult for me. I'm not happy about it. When you have a farm, you *have* to think about your neighbours. I think our maize is too close to Dave and Jenny's crop. But it's been hard for Dad and Helen this last year. They haven't earned much money. The GM crop trial has given them a new start.'

'Anna says it's nearly too late,' Joe said. 'The maize is almost in flower.'

'You like her, don't you?' Kate asked.

'I don't know,' he replied. He looked at Kate, his face serious. 'Yes, you're right. I like her a lot. She thinks I'm boring because I go surfing.'

Kate went very quiet.

'But does she like you?' she asked at last.

'I don't know,' Joe replied. 'No, probably not much.'

The sun was low over the sea now, and it was beginning to turn the surf deep red. The air was still warm. The beach was almost empty but the sea was still full of surfers. Kate touched Joe's arm.

'Come on!' she shouted. 'I'll race you into the water.'

Soon they were riding high on the top of a big wave. Just for that one special minute, time stopped – and Anna and GM vegetables weren't important.

Chapter 4   The Lie

Anna wasn't interested in the protesters.

'Yes, I saw them,' she said. 'I couldn't spend my time hiding under a stupid vegetable head! You know how strongly I feel about GM crops, Joe. We talked about it a lot last week. I want everybody to know who I am. Then I can tell them what *I* think!'

'But it was a great idea,' Joe replied. 'A lot of people stopped to ask questions. They took away a lot of information.'

'Questions! Questions!' Anna said angrily. 'It's too late to ask questions! While everybody's asking questions, that GM maize is almost in flower. Don't you understand, Joe? It's time to *do* something.'

She looked at Joe, her face now more serious than angry.

'Let's go for a walk,' she said. 'I'll get my jacket.'

The air was very fresh down by the stream where Joe waited for Anna. Further along the stream he could see an old wooden bridge. People were sitting there, with their feet in the water.

Joe and Anna walked across the bridge and made their way towards Cloud Hill. It was a long climb to the top. The wind was stronger up there. Clouds ran across the sky, throwing large shadows over the fields below them. At Tregonnan Farm they could see Dave trying to throw a ball to Fin with his left arm. Jenny was watering the pots of flowers outside the kitchen door. They seemed very small and unimportant and a long way away.

'I love Cornwall as much as Jenny and Dave,' Anna said. 'My grandmother was born on a farm on the other side of Newquay. That's why I wanted to come back here.'

Anna walked away from him. Joe watched her as she disappeared down the other side of the hill.

'Where are you going?' he shouted.

'Follow me and you'll find out!' Anna called to him. 'Come on. It's not far.'

Joe ran after Anna. When he reached the bottom of the hill, Anna was already climbing over a low stone wall. On the other side of the wall was a large, new-looking sign which said: PRIVATE LAND.

They were standing right in the middle of a field of maize. Joe suddenly realized where they were.

'This is the GM maize!' he said. 'It looks just the same as my aunt and uncle's.'

'Of course it does!' Anna said. 'What did you imagine? Black and grey plants like those silly vegetables in the protest?'

'I don't know,' Joe said. 'Why are there wooden sticks down the middle of the crop?'

'One half is GM, the other one isn't,' Anna explained. 'Scientists test them both. They have to produce results for the government.'

'That's good, surely,' Joe said.

Anna moved closer to Joe, until her face was next to his. He half-closed his eyes and waited.

'I want to ask you something,' Anna said quietly. 'You must promise not to . . .'

'Hi, Joe, what are you doing here?'

Kate's voice came from behind them. They turned round in surprise.

'Hi, Kate,' Joe said. 'This is Anna. We've been for a walk on Cloud Hill.'

Anna and Kate looked at each other in silence. Anna spoke first.

'What's it like, living on a GM farm?' Her voice was hard.

Anna took hold of one of the maize plants and bent it between her fingers.

'Do you realize that this plant will be in flower next week?' she asked. 'Do you know how much pollen it will produce?'

'No, not exactly,' Kate replied. 'Why should I?'

'Because this plant is genetically different, that's why,' Anna said. 'And the wind will carry its pollen over to Dave and Jenny's organic maize and they won't be able to sell it.'

'You don't know that,' Kate said.

'Even if that doesn't happen,' Anna said, 'there's another problem. How do you know GM maize won't be bad for you in the future? Or for the animals that eat it?'

'My father trusts the scientists,' Kate said.

'I don't,' Anna replied. 'They make mistakes.'

'There are a lot of people like you who come here,' Kate said. She laughed unkindly. 'You don't have *all* the answers. You're not a scientist. Why don't you ask *me* what I think? I was at the protest last week. Where were *you*?'

Anna threw the maize plant onto the ground and walked angrily away.

'It's too late for protesting,' she shouted.

'She has very strong opinions, doesn't she?' Kate said.

'Yes,' Joe agreed, 'but you do too. So *you* were the potato with the green eyes! Why didn't you tell me?'

'I don't need to talk about it,' Kate replied. 'I take action.'

'You both talk a lot of sense and I still don't know what I think,' Joe said. 'I'm glad I've seen you. I planned to phone you when I got back. It's a good day for surfing. I'm free after five o'clock. Do you want to go?'

'Great,' Kate replied. 'I'll take you in my car. See you later, Joe.'

He ran after Anna.

'Can't you talk about GM crops without being so rude?' he asked. 'You didn't *have* to go to the Ladocks' farm. And we were on their land!'

Anna continued walking and Joe had to hurry after her again.

'What did you want to ask me?' he said.

Anna stopped.

'Are you free tonight?' she asked.

'No,' Joe replied. 'I've just agreed to go surfing with Kate. Why didn't you ask me earlier? Is it important?'

'Important?' Anna cried. 'Just a matter of life and death, that's all!'

And she refused to say any more.

♦

It was fun at Fistral Beach. Joe only had one problem. He fell off his surfboard a number of times. After he hit his face on it twice, Kate told him to stop.

'The best surfer is the one who's having fun,' she said. 'That's

Anna threw the maize plant onto the ground.

what my teacher in Hawaii told me. Surfing isn't a test, Joe. It's all about the sun, the sea – and friends.'

It was nearly dark as they drove out of Newquay. The moon was low over the sea.

'Look at all those beautiful stars!' Joe said. 'We can't see them clearly in London because there are too many streetlights.'

Close to Tregonnan Farm, they came to the bridge over the stream.

'Isn't that Anna?' Joe asked. 'Look, down there, near the bridge! Let's stop.'

It was Anna. She was with a group of people. One of them, a man with long dark hair, was opening a map. He ran his finger along it and called to his friends down by the stream. They didn't notice Kate's car on the other side of the bridge.

'Perhaps they're lost,' Kate said. 'Do you think we should offer to help?'

'No,' Joe said. 'I saw her with him in Newquay last Sunday. They seem very friendly. Let's go back the other way.'

'Don't you want her to see us together?' Kate asked, laughing. 'I've seen some of those people before.' She became more serious. 'I'm sure I know the one with the map – Anna's friend. His picture was in the newspaper, but I can't remember why.'

Kate turned the car round and they took the main road. Dave and Jenny were already in bed. Joe was glad because he didn't want to talk.

Joe lay awake for a long time. He couldn't stop thinking about Anna and the way she smiled at the man with long brown hair.

'I trust Kate more than I trust Anna,' he thought sadly, 'but I'd still like to go out with Anna. I'll ask her tomorrow.'

◆

The next morning, Anna sang as she worked. She worked quickly at her side of the field and then came to help Joe.

Anna was with a group of people.

'Do you want to go to the cinema tonight?' Joe asked.

'Thanks, Joe, but I'm busy,' she replied.

'Are you going out with the people you were with last night?' Joe asked. 'You seem to know them well.'

'Who do you mean?' Anna asked.

'Near the bridge,' Joe said. 'We passed you on our way back. Kate wanted to stop.'

'It wasn't me,' Anna said quickly.

'Of course it was!' he said. 'Your hair was shining in the dark.'

'There are other girls around here with fair hair, Joe,' she said.

'But not as beautiful as yours,' Joe replied.

'You've made a mistake,' Anna said, her face red. 'Perhaps you were too busy looking at Kate.'

Anna stopped singing after this conversation, and she stopped helping Joe.

'Why is she lying?' Joe thought. 'What's she hiding? I was right! I *can't* trust her!'

Joe was still thinking about Anna when he went into the kitchen. His feelings for her were different now, and he was sad about that. 'I'll talk to her about it,' he thought.

'Why don't we eat in the garden?' Dave said. 'It's too hot to be inside. You take the drinks, Joe. I can carry the bowl of salad with one hand.'

'Did you see those people down by the bridge last night?' Joe asked. 'One of the men had long brown hair.'

'No,' Dave replied. 'We get a lot of visitors at this time of the year. People often stop at the bridge because it's so pretty by the stream.'

'So you climbed Cloud Hill?' Jenny said as she came out to join them. 'Anna told me.'

'It was just an excuse to show me the GM maize,' Joe said.

'You went into the Ladocks' field?' Jenny asked, surprised. 'Ken Ladock won't like that. He's had a lot of trouble from protesters in the last few weeks. They stand on the wall and shout. I can hear them sometimes. Keep away from his farm, Joe. It's not safe.'

As they sat talking, the wind became stronger. Dark clouds covered the moon.

'I can smell rain,' Dave said.

Soon a light rain began to fall.

'Time to go inside,' Jenny said.

Joe helped to wash the dishes. The rain was loud against the kitchen window and storm clouds filled the sky. From time to time, forks of lightning lit Cloud Hill and the fields around it.

'I hope Anna's all right,' Jenny said. 'Her tent is very close to the stream. The water's already too high because of the rain last week.'

'She must come into the house,' Dave said. 'I'll go and get her now.'

'I think she's going out,' Joe said. 'But perhaps she's changed her mind. I'll go. I need to talk to her.'

Dave and Jenny looked at Joe and smiled.

The wind pushed Joe all the way down to the stream. Rain poured over his face. He couldn't see anything until he noticed the small light inside Anna's tent.

'Anna!' he called. 'We want you to come to the house until the storm ends!'

'I'm OK,' she shouted. 'Don't worry about me.'

'I'm not going back without you!' Joe shouted above the wind. 'Come on! The water has almost reached your tent.'

There was a long silence. At last Anna came outside, looking frightened and nervous.

'I'm busy, Joe,' she said. 'Leave me alone.'

'Why did you lie to me?' Joe asked angrily. 'You *were* near that bridge yesterday!'

'Don't look at me like that!' Anna replied. 'It was easier to lie, that's all. You won't understand.'

'Understand what?' Joe asked.

'Can I trust you?' Anna asked. 'Will you promise not to repeat what I'm going to tell you?'

'OK,' Joe said. 'Now tell me what's happening.'

'Those people by the bridge last night were the ones who trashed the GM crop near Bodmin Moor. I'm going with them tonight. We're going to trash the Ladocks' maize.' Before Joe could reply, Anna touched his arm. 'Come with us,' she said.

Anna's face looked so hopeful in the half light that Joe went cold.

'I'm sorry, Anna,' Joe said, 'but I can't break the law.'

'The GM scientists are the criminals,' Anna replied. 'You feel sorry for Dave and Jenny, don't you? Will you help us or not?'

'I don't like what the Ladocks are doing,' Joe explained. 'But that doesn't give me the right to trash their crops.'

'You won't come because you like Kate,' Anna replied. 'You don't want to hurt *her*! I'm right, aren't I?'

'I'm not coming with you because it's wrong, Anna,' Joe said.

A fork of lightning lit up the sky. Joe saw that Anna's face was wet with rain or tears.

'And *you* mustn't go either!' he shouted. 'It's criminal and dangerous. They sometimes send protesters to prison. I don't want that to happen to you.'

'Don't forget your promise,' Anna said.

'Is that all you can say?' Joe asked. 'OK, I'll keep my promise. I won't tell anybody, not even Kate. But I'm not coming with you and I won't change my mind. Don't ask me again.'

'I won't,' Anna said. 'You'll see that I'm right in a few years' time. But it will be too late.'

Joe walked away.

'Good luck,' he said, 'and be careful.'

'Am I doing the right thing?' he asked himself all the way back to the house. 'I don't know,' was his only answer.

Chapter 5   Trouble in the Fields

'Anna's OK,' Joe told his aunt and uncle as water ran off him onto the kitchen floor.

'Now I'm telling lies,' he thought.

'I wouldn't like to be out there on a night like this,' Jenny said. 'Thanks for going, Joe. You must take off those wet clothes.'

'I think I'll go to bed,' Joe replied. 'Goodnight.'

Joe didn't try to sleep. He wanted to go out into the storm again and stop Anna. She was in danger and he wanted to help her. Then, suddenly, he thought of Kate. 'Her parents will lose a lot of money because of me!'

Joe felt sick at the thought. He went to the window and looked out. Where *was* Anna? What were they all doing out there? Were the other people just using her? Did they plan to run away and leave her after this?

The lightning moved away and the fields became suddenly dark again. Joe lay on the bed and waited. His eyes closed for a few minutes, long enough to have a terrible dream. A wave taller than Cloud Hill was coming quickly towards him. It knocked him from his surfboard and he turned over and over under the water. Then everything went black.

Joe opened his eyes. His face was wet and his hands were shaking. He was reaching for the light switch when a blue light lit up the night sky. Was it the lightning again? He got out of bed and went over to the window.

The Ladocks' farm was completely lit up. Lights shone outside the house, next to the maize crop – everywhere! They seemed to turn round and round in the black sky.

They were the lights of police cars.

At the same time, Joe heard his aunt and uncle in the garden below him. He moved quickly away from the window, but he was too late.

31

'Come down, Joe!' Dave shouted. 'Somebody's trashing the Ladocks' crop! The police have just arrived.'

Joe pulled on his jeans and a shirt and made his way slowly downstairs. But he really wanted to go back to sleep. He wanted to forget that this was happening.

The wind carried the sound of angry voices across the fields.

'I know it's wrong, but I'm pleased,' Jenny said, excited.

'It's a big field,' Dave said. 'Did they trash it all, do you think? I hope so! I've thought about going there and . . .'

'Dave!' Jenny said.

'It's OK,' Dave said. 'I couldn't do that. The Ladocks have had a hard time.'

'Anna asked me to help her,' Joe said quietly.

There was a long silence.

'*Anna's* there? And you *knew* about this?' Dave asked in surprise.

'Yes,' Joe replied. 'She told me just before she went to meet the others. They were the protesters who trashed the crop near Bodmin Moor.'

'She works for us, Joe,' Jenny said. 'Why didn't you stop her?'

'I tried,' Joe said, 'but she didn't listen. She's an adult, Aunt Jenny. She can choose.'

'But why didn't you tell us?' Jenny asked again.

'I promised Anna,' Joe said. 'But I didn't really know what she was planning then. It was very stupid of me. I had to keep my promise.'

'Well, it's too late now,' Dave said. 'Let's go in and have a cup of tea.'

As they went into the house, Joe looked back at the police lights. They were moving away from the Ladocks' house now. They became smaller as the cars turned through the gate at the bottom of the hill. Then they disappeared. Everything was dark again, except for a light in the farmhouse.

Suddenly, the moon came out and lit up the valley and it was

32

'Come down, Joe!' Dave shouted.

beautiful again. The only sound came from Fin running around the garden.

'Why didn't the Ladocks leave their sheep in that field!' Joe thought sadly.

As he followed his aunt and uncle into the kitchen, the telephone rang. Jenny answered it.

'We'll come in the morning,' Jenny said, putting the telephone down. She turned to Dave and Joe. 'They're keeping all of them at the police station until morning. The police will talk to them then.'

♦

The sound of voices woke Joe up. One of them was Kate's. Joe looked at his watch. It was ten o'clock. The light coming through his window was cold and grey. He got dressed quickly and went downstairs. Kate was in the kitchen with a worried-looking man. Anna stood opposite them. Her clothes and her hair were dirty and there were dark shadows under her eyes.

When Joe came into the room, Kate turned towards him, her eyes angry.

'This is my father!' she shouted. 'Does he look like the sort of man who wants to destroy this farm? He trusts the government. He believes that GM crops are a good idea. Now you've got what you want. But what has he got! Nothing! Why didn't you tell us about their plans?'

'I'm sorry,' Joe said, surprised. 'But I promised Anna.'

Mr Ladock looked coldly at Joe.

'That's no excuse,' he said. 'Everybody has the right to protest. But nobody has the right to destroy other people's crops. They don't have the right to break the law.'

'You're love-sick, Joe,' Kate said. 'That's why you didn't say anything. I really liked you! But now I never want to see you again! Never!' Kate stopped in the open door. 'And why didn't they keep *you* in *prison*!' she shouted at Anna.

'I'm sorry, Ken,' Dave said. 'I didn't know anything about this. If Joe . . .'

'I believe you,' Mr Ladock replied, 'but I've lost that crop now. That's a lot of money. You know how difficult it is for farms these days.' He looked at Anna. 'I'll see you at the trial, young lady.'

He followed Kate out to her car and they drove away.

'We trashed the crop before the police arrived,' Anna said happily.

'Who told them?' Joe asked.

'Mrs Ladock,' Anna replied. 'The storm woke her. She got up to close a window.'

'You'll have to stay in England until your trial,' Dave said. 'What about your course? Term starts in September!'

'I *had* to do it,' Anna replied. Suddenly there were tears in her eyes.

Jenny went over to Anna and put her arm around Anna's shoulders.

'I know,' she said. 'We're pleased that the GM crop has gone. But you can't solve everybody's problems, love. We're worried about *you*. What are your parents going to say?'

'Mum will understand,' Anna said, 'but I'm not sure about Dad.' She smiled at Joe. 'Thanks for keeping your promise. Do you think Kate is *really* angry with you?'

'You heard what she said,' Joe replied. 'I'll try to talk to her again.'

'That's brave of you,' Jenny said.

'Not brave,' Joe thought. 'She's a good friend. I don't want to lose her.'

♦

The next few days were the longest of Joe's life. He missed Kate. And, for the first time in his life, he didn't want to go surfing. He and Anna worked hard, but they didn't talk very much.

'I don't know why you're so angry with me,' she said one morning. 'I'm the one who's in trouble.'

'I'm not angry with you,' Joe said. 'I miss Kate.'

'Why don't you go and see her then?' Anna asked. 'You'll feel better if you talk to her.'

'It's too soon,' Joe said.

'It isn't!' Anna said. 'Go now!'

Joe got into his car and drove straight to the Ladocks' farm. Ken Ladock and his wife both came to the door, unsmiling.

'I'm surprised to see you, Joe,' Ken Ladock said, 'after what you've done.'

'You're not welcome here,' Helen Ladock said.

'I understand that,' Joe said. 'But can you please tell Kate that I *must* talk to her? I'll wait for her in the car.'

Kate came out immediately.

'We've nothing to talk about, Joe.'

'I'm really sorry I couldn't tell you,' he replied. 'You know that.'

'I know that you're selfish,' she said quietly. 'You were thinking about Anna, not about us.'

Now Joe was angry. 'Me, selfish?' he cried. 'How can you say that? Listen, Kate. I kept a promise to a friend, that's all.'

Kate's face looked softer.

'I think that Anna was very brave,' he continued. 'Wrong, but brave. She believed she was right. And I believed I was right too. You'll have to accept that.'

'Why?'

'Because I want us to be friends,' Joe said. 'Can you forgive me?'

'How can I?' Kate said at last.

There was a long silence between them.

'I've decided to accept a job in Newquay,' Kate told him. 'Then I can help Dad and Helen too. It's going to be difficult for them to make the farm a success after this.'

'What about their other fields?'

'You're not welcome here,' Helen Ladock said.

'They'll have a crop of vegetables in the autumn. That will earn them some money,' Kate said.

'You haven't answered my first question yet,' Joe said again.

'I don't know, Joe,' Kate replied. 'You don't think you were wrong. That's the problem.'

'I do,' Joe said. 'It's wrong to trash somebody's crops. It's *not* wrong to keep a promise! But I made a bad mistake. I didn't ask Anna enough questions first. Will you forgive me?'

'OK,' Kate said. 'But Dad and Helen won't.'

'Thanks, Kate,' Joe said quietly.

'When are you going back to London?' she asked.

'In about three weeks' time,' Joe replied. He looked around him. 'I can't believe I'm saying this . . . I shall miss the farm and the sea.'

'And Anna?' Kate asked.

'I don't know,' Joe said. 'But I don't think so.'

'It's a pity you're leaving so soon,' Kate said. 'The surf is much better in September and it's quieter.'

'I'll have to come back at weekends,' he said. 'Let's go surfing now, Kate.'

She shook her head. 'I don't want to leave Dad and Helen.'

'But it's not much fun alone!' Joe said. 'Remember?'

'OK,' Kate agreed, laughing. 'I'll come – but only if you promise me one thing.'

'I always keep my promises,' Joe said. 'You know that!'

'Promise me you won't try so hard!' Kate replied. 'Just enjoy it. Please!'

'I promise,' Joe said.

He looked into Kate's eyes. He realized for the first time that they were even greener than Anna's. And the look on her face was full of trust.

'Surfing is about the sun, the sea – and friends,' he said softly.

ACTIVITIES

Chapter 1

Before you read

1 Look at the Word List at the back of this book. Which words can you use to discuss farming?

2 Read the Introduction to the book and then discuss these questions.

    a Why are GM crops a problem for Joe's aunt and uncle?

    b Are there any organic farms where you live? Do you grow or eat organic vegetables? Why (not)?

    c Are there any GM crops where you live? Do you think they are a good or bad idea? Give reasons for your answer.

While you read

3 Are these sentences right (✓) or wrong (✗)?

    a Joe is going on holiday with Tom. .....

    b Joe's uncle needs help on his farm. .....

    c Tregonnan Farm grows GM crops. .....

    d Joe's uncle's farm is near the sea. .....

    e Newquay has the best surfing beaches in the country. .....

    f Joe enjoys surfing. .....

    g His uncle and aunt have no other help on their farm. .....

    h Joe's new surfboard is heavy. .....

    i The farm at the bottom of Cloud Hill is a sheep farm. .....

    j The Ladocks are growing GM maize. .....

    k Joe doesn't eat meat. .....

    l Joe has to get up at seven o'clock. .....

After you read

4 Who is talking? Who or what are they talking about?

    a 'I fell over the dog.'

    b 'You haven't got any other plans now.'

    c 'This one's better because it's so light.'

    d 'They bought the farm last year.'

    e 'They taste much better.'

    f 'I hate it here!'

5 Discuss what you know about each of these people.

Joe   Jenny   Dave   Tom   Joe's mother

6 Work with another student and have this telephone conversation.

Student A: You are Joe. Tell Tom about your new holiday plans. How are you feeling.

Student B: You are Tom. Ask Joe questions. Tell him what he should do.

Chapter 2

Before you read

7 Discuss these questions.

a Are there many shops where you live? Which ones do you like best?

b Where can you buy organic vegetable?

While you read

8 Complete these sentences.

a Jenny and Joe take boxes of .... to Newquay.

b In Newquay, there are .... shops in every street.

c Joe enjoys .... two hamburgers with cheese.

d He meets a girl who is staying on her parents' ....

e She also enjoys ....

f Joe's aunt looks .... when she sees Kate.

g At the farm, Anna is having .... with Joe's uncle.

h While they eat, they all discuss .... crops.

i Anna doesn't seem to be .... in surfing.

j She thinks that Kate is their ....

After you read

9 Discuss these statements from the story.

a 'New ideas usually frighten people.'

b 'Perhaps we should just use GM crops safely.'

c 'Is there any place for organic food . . . in this science fiction future?'

Chapter 3

Before you read

10 Discuss these questions.

    a What do people protest about in your country?

    b What do you think about protests? Are they useful?

While you read

11 Who or what are they?

    a **It** looks beautiful in the sun. ....

    b **It** is very busy because the weather is so good. ....

    c **It** walks slowly up to Joe. ....

    d **She** is talking to a man with long brown hair. ....

    e **She** buys a surfboard. ....

    f **They** are all watching and waiting for the perfect wave. ....

    g **He** falls off his surfboard. ....

    h **She** has green eyes. ....

After you read

12 Describe Joe's visit to Fistral Beach. Discuss:

    a the beach

    b Joe's surfing

    c Kate's feelings

13 Describe the sport of surfing. What do you need when you surf? What do you do? Why do you think people enjoy it?

14 Joe asks Kate: 'What do you think about your father's crop trial?' What does Kate answer? Do you understand the Ladocks' problem? What should they do?

Chapter 4

Before you read

15 How do you think Joe feels about Kate and Anna? Which of them does he prefer? Why?

16 Is it ever right to tell a lie? Do you tell lies? Why (not)?

17 What do they say? Circle the correct answers.

    a 'It's too late to ask ..... .'

       answers   people   questions

    b 'It's time to ..... something'

       do   make   learn

    c 'One half is GM, the other half isn't. Scientists ..... them both.'

       test   eat   try

    d 'My father ..... the scientists.'

       likes   hates   trusts

    e 'It's too late for ..... .'

       talking   protesting   testing

    f 'Important? Just a matter of life and ....., that's all.'

       love   death   protest

    g 'I've ..... some of those people before.'

       seen   met   helped

    h 'Why is she .....? What's she hiding?'

       doing   looking   lying

    i '..... away from his farm, Joe. It's not safe.'

       Keep   Go   Stay

    j 'We're going to ..... the Ladocks' maize.'

       grow   visit   trash

After you read

18 Read these answers. What are the questions?

    a 'Follow me and you'll find out.'

    b 'No, not exactly. Why should I?'

    c 'I don't need to talk about it.'

    d 'No, I've just agreed to go surfing with Kate.'

    e 'It was just an excuse to show me the GM maize.'

    f 'You don't want to hurt *her*. I'm right, aren't I?'

Chapter 5

19 Discuss these questions.

    a Do you think it is ever right to destroy a farmer's crop?

    b How should people protest if they don't like the idea of GM crops?

While you read

20 Circle the correct words to complete the sentences.

    a Joe dreams about *surfing / protesters*.

    b The Ladocks' maize crop is *destroyed / saved*.

    c At that time Anna is *in her tent / at the farm*.

    d Joe tells his aunt and uncle about Anna *before / after* the police arrive.

    e Kate is *angry / pleased* about the protestors' actions.

    f Anna will return to Sweden *immediately / later than she planned*.

    g Joe thinks that he *made / didn't make* a mistake.

    h Kate and Joe *will / will not* surf together again.

21 Correct the sentences that are untrue.

    a Joe lies to his aunt and uncle.

    b Joe trashes the GM crops with Anna.

    c Anna stays at the police station until the next morning.

    d Mr Ladock trusts the government.

    e Joe will always be welcome at the Ladocks' farm.

    f Joe misses Kate after the trashing.

22 Describe the attack on the Ladock's farm. Discuss:

    a the weather

    b the actions of the protestors

    c the Ladocks' feelings

    d Joe's feelings

23 Have this conversation at the police station.

    Student A: You are a police officer. Ask Anna questions about the trashing of the Ladocks' crop.

    Student B: You are Anna. Answer the police officer's questions.

Writing

24 Write a short newspaper report about the trashing of the Ladocks' GM crop. Describe the Ladocks' feelings. Explain what will happen now to the protestors.

25 This story is about a GM crop trial. Explain the purpose of the trials. What are the possible problems?

26 Jenny and Dave have written to their local newspaper and their local politician about the GM crop trial. Write one of these letters, giving their opinions.

27 Imagine that you work for Newquay's tourist office. Write a page for the *Newquay Daily Times* or for the Internet about surfing holidays in Newquay.

28 You are Anna. Write a letter home. Tell your family what has happened.

29 What does this story tell us about Joe and Tom; Anna and Joe; Kate and Joe? What does each person feel about the other?

30 'The best answer to problems is to talk about them.' Do you agree? Why (not)?

31 Which of the people in the story do you like best/least? Explain why.

Answers for the Activities in this book are available from the Penguin Readers website. A free Activity Worksheet is also available from the website. Activity Worksheets are part of the Penguin Teacher Support Programme, which also includes Progress Tests and Graded Reader Guidelines. For more information, please visit: www.penguinreaders.com.